The Wonder in Alice
by Kate Brennan

Copyright © 2025 by Kate Brennan

1st Ed. August 14, 2025

Cover art by Wrenee Murphy.

All rights reserved.

No portion of this book may be reproduced in any form without written permission from the publisher or author, except as permitted by U.S. copyright law.

This play may not be fed into any LLM or other AI software for any reason whatsoever.

The Wonder in Alice premiered at DreamWrights Center for Community Arts in York, PA on September 26, 2025. It was directed by Gregory DeCandia. The original cast included:

ADDI - Marley Bell / Camryn McCormick
LOQI - Anja Homberger / Sheridan Lowery
IMAGIN - Ashlynn Leedy / Ella Jack
CURI - Lorelei Drinkut / Brooklyn Chambers
EX/ QUEEN/ LOUDSPEAKER - Andrew Texter

RINA/ WHITE RABBIT– Sadie Jarmer
EDI/ WHITE RABBIT – Mylah Schmitt
CHARLIE/ WHITE RABBIT– Soren Paleshi
BEAU/ WHITE RABBIT – Leo Crone

THE MAD HATTER/ TEACHER – Sarah Garber
THE CHESHIRE CAT/ JANITOR – Ruoxia Li
THE CATERPILLAR/ LIBRARIAN – Anastasia Rosenbrien

THE ENSEMBLE
Elizabeth Baker, Mary Baker, Olivia Baker, Briana C. Brindley, Sarah Crowther, Isabella Evans, Harper Guise, Juliette Guise, Elyssa Jack, Lacey Jarmer, Luna Jolley, Hannah Keilholtz, Audrey Anne Kveragas, Amy Kyles, Ramona Line, William Line, Lilyanna Martin, Vada McClair, Charlotte Melnyk, Devin Moyer, Adelaide Myers, Shanell Nelson, Arvin Paleshi (Vial), Lucy Thompson (Bunny), Sarah Urand

INSTALLATION ARTISTS
RABBIT HOLE: Annelise Vuono & the Dreams in a Jar Mural Arts Camp
CHESHIRE CAT: The Nevin Family: Gretchen, Roo, Jack, Phillip & Riley Sue
CATERPILLAR: Sarah Noble & the students of Logos Academy
MAD HATTER'S HALL: Gregory & Iggy DeCandia
QUEEN'S COURT: DeMond B. Nason & the Building Wonderland Camp

CREATIVE TEAM
ARTISTIC DIRECTOR/DIRECTOR: Gregory DeCandia
EXECUTIVE DIRECTOR: Eric Miller
ASSISTANT DIRECTOR: Lily Ganong
PRODUCTION STAGE MANAGERS: Anna Fraser & Katelyn Moyer
ASSISTANT STAGE MANAGER: Adi Sweitzer
SET DESIGNER: Crystal Ganong
COSTUME DESIGNER: Kristen Fraser
SOUND DESIGNER: Trim Walker
PROJECTION DESIGNER: DeMond B. Nason
PROPERTIES: Iris Lewin

CREW: Kevin Keith Allen (Master of Bunnemonies), Dee Dee Allen, Lukas Cooper, Alison Conrad, Naomi Cooke, Lukas Cooper, Bennet Crone, Millie Crone, Rebecca Eastman, Amy Eyler, Casper Ganong, Sawyer Hill, Joanna Miller, Natalie Montejo, Dawn Oswald, Nevaeh Pineda, Rodd Robertson, Audrey Yabut

CHARACTERS

ADDI- Adventurous Alice, most likely to take a dare or get injured
LOQI- Loquacious Alice, has an expansive vocabulary, really likes to talk things out
IMAGIN - Imaginative Alice, a dreamer and visionary
CURI - Curious Alice, loves to ask questions; it sometimes gets her in trouble
EX - Expressive Alice, feels all the things
    Also plays THE QUEEN & THE LOUDSPEAKER

Note on the Alices - Alices can be any age or gender with a preference for Addi to be who we first envision as quintessentially Alice.

RINA/ WHITE RABBIT– an overachieving classmate, later a rabbit
EDI/ WHITE RABBIT – a mischievous classmate, later, a rabbit
CHARLIE/ WHITE RABBIT– a quick classmate, later, a rabbit
BEAU/ WHITE RABBIT – a terrified classmate, later, a rabbit
    WHITE RABBIT– a messenger, servant to the queen

THE MAD HATTER – a whacky hatter who runs a never-ending tea party
    ALSO plays THE TEACHER

THE CHESHIRE CAT – a cool poet cat who only speaks in haiku
    ALSO plays THE JANITOR

THE CATERPILLAR – a hungry insect who prefers iambic pentameter
        ALSO plays THE LIBRARIAN

THE ENSEMBLE, any age, any gender, 12+ members

The Ensemble Members also play the following –
    MB - The Master of Bunnemonies
    VIAL – a vial who says "drink me."
    STUDENTS
    BUNNIES
    LIBRARY AIDES
    THE BODY OF THE CHESHIRE CAT
    THE BODY OF THE CATERPILLAR
    THE MAD HATTERS

SETTING
Alice's ever-wandering, ever-curious head where anything and everything is possible and nothing is what it seems.

NOTE ON THE TEXT
The world is extremely playful, magical and whimsical and requires only bodies in space and the magic of theatre. Use the talents of the cast, use fabric, use flashlights. Use shadow and puppetry. This is theatre of the mind at its finest.

NOTE ON THE ENSEMBLE
The Ensemble assembles the world around the Alices. They may speak and physicalize The Cheshire Cat/Caterpillar, but the manifestation of these characters will be left to the creativity of the ensemble and the vision and discretion of the director. Please divide & allocate group lines if it serves you.

NOTE ON THE SHOW
The show has two complimentary elements.

1. In the lobby, there is a letter-writing station, "Advice to a Young Caterpillar" with the question: "What kindness would you write to your younger self?" Each night, these letters are collected and collaged to create Alice's last letter within the show.

2. There is an invitation to extend the world of the show beyond the stage into the larger building by commissioning local artists to create experiential art installations a la Meow Wolf. The themes for the premiere production were: Rabbit Hole, Cheshire Cat, Caterpillar, Mad Hatter's Hall & Queen's Court.

SYNOPSIS
A brand new take on the whimsical classic, with five Alices at its epicenter. Advice to a young caterpillar in play form.

SECTIONS
Part 1: What Alice Forgot
PART 2: Five Alices Wearing the Same Dress
PART 3: A my Name is Alice
PART 4: The Hall of Doors
PART 5: Drink Me
Part 6: Cheshire Cat Smile
PART 7: Advice from a Caterpillar
PART 8: We're All Mad Here
PART 9: Go Ask Alice
PART 10: Alice All Along

PROLOGUE
MB, the Master of Bunnemonies, enters with a very unenthusiastic helper Bunny. S/he addresses the audience.

                    MB
"Two households, both alike in dignity—"
No no, that's not how we begin!
This is the portion of the program
Where we're meant to welcome you in!

                    BUNNY
                    Welcome.

                    MB
"It was the best of times, it was the worst of times—"
No <clap> that's not it again
I suppose we should say something about Exits
And Who and Where and When

                    BUNNY
                    In the case of an emergency,
                    please note that the closest
                    exit may be behind you.

                    MB
"Happy families are all alike—"
Why do I continue to confound?!
Here we're meant to tell you
Turn off things that make sound

                    BUNNY
                <Phone sound.>

                      MB
Now if you would –-

The Bunny tugs the MB's attire, then hands the MB a note.

Ah–!

(This note may contain any information that your organization needs to communicate – sponsors, upcoming events, how to subscribe, special thanks etc.)

MB reads note aloud to audience and hands it back to Bunny.

                    MB (cont.)
Thank you.

Now… if you would, please…
Sit up, enjoy, and join us to be inspired
Ah, yes,… this is how we begin:

                   MB & BUNNY
"Alice was beginning –…"

Immediately into–

1: WHAT ALICE FORGOT

Darkness.
Spotlight.
The Ensemble conjures Alice.

                    MB/ ENSEMBLE:
Ahhhhhhlice.

                                     Alice appears.
Ahhhhhhhhhlice.
          Alice watches a single letter fall from the sky.
Ahhhhhhhhhhhlice.
                         Alice reaches for the letter.

A book snaps shut on the letter as lights come up abruptly:

                    ALL
ALICE!

Suddenly, a classroom. RINA, EDI, CHARLIE & BEAU, along with other children, scribble furiously at their desks, heads down. Adventurous Alice (ADDI), F, any age to play a child, stands atop a desk, out of sorts and out of place.

What a surprise.

                    ADDI
Yes? What? Yes?
Did someone say something?

LOUDSPEAKER
WHAT do you think you're doing?

The rest of the children are writing at their desks.

ADDI
I am trying to figure out what to write. For my letter.

LOUDSPEAKER
And standing on top of a desk is going to help you do that, *how*?

ADDI
There was a letter – my letter, it was falling and I thought if I could just –

LOUDSPEAKER
Will you all please focus on your assignment until your new teacher arrives?

ADDI
But I –

LOUDSPEAKER
Would you take your seat, child?

ADDI
Yes, Principal Reine.
She gets down and picks up her seat.
Where would you like me to take it?

                    LOUDSPEAKER
SIIIIIIIIIIILENCE!
Loudspeaker clicks off. Addi rushes to her seat.

Children scribble furiously. Addi is uninspired.

The JANITOR opens the door to empty the trash. Addi is right next to the door.

                    ADDI
Hi, Mr./Ms. Mao.
I'm feeling uninspired.

                    JANITOR
Have you been searching?
Sometimes you must be lost in
Order to be found

The Janitor empties the trash and exits.

                    ADDI
Thanks, Mr./Ms. Mao.

                    RINA
Shhhhh!

Addi slinks down to the floor.

                    ADDI
I don't really know what that means.

RINA
What are you doing? You should be in your seat.

ADDI
I'm looking for something.

EDI
What?

ADDI
Inspiration.

EDI
I don't think you're going to find it down there.

RINA
We are *supposed* to be working on our *letters*, or have you forgotten?

ADDI
I know. I am. I'm just – I'm having trouble–

BEAU
Who's in trouble?

ADDI
I'm in trouble. I had it. I thought I had it. I was so close.

CHARLIE
Close to what?

                        ADDI
My letter, or, I dunno,– the idea for the letter. It was right at my fingertips.

                        CHARLIE
I'm almost done mine.

                        ADDI
You are?!

                        RINA
You two shouldn't be out of your seats! The new teacher will be here any –

THE NEW TEACHER (later the Mad Hatter) bursts into the room like a magical tornado.

                        TEACHER
Why is a raven like a writing desk?

Good morning, all!

The students freeze, unsure of what to do.

(Chastising him/herself) No no no. First "Good Morning, all!" then "Why is a raven like a writing desk?"

Let's try that again, shall we?

Clap.

The teacher exits.
No one breathes.

                        EDI
Did that just happen?

The teacher bursts back into the room exactly as before.

                      TEACHER
Good morning, all!

Why is a raven like a writing desk?

Stunned silence.

Did I do it wrong again–? No, no. Nonono. I got it right that time:
>   first, "good morning, all"
>   then, "why is a raven like a writing desk?"

Nothing.

Perhaps they didn't hear:
WHY IS A RAVEN LIKE A WRITING DESK?

The teacher begins to unburden herself/himself of things.

Hmmm? Guesses? Conjectures? Curiosities?

No response.

Oh dear. Oh dear. Is this — this is the classroom, is it not? A place to learn things? To ask questions? To debate big ideas?

No response.

TEACHER
Oh no. This will not do. This will not do at all. All wrong. All wrongallwrongallwrongallwrong.

The teacher reverses order, repacks him/herself and exits.

The students are confused.

RINA
Should we get someone?

EDI
What in the world —

BEAU
This is the most interesting class I've ever had.

The teacher enters a third time, just the same as before.

TEACHER
Good morning, all! Why is a raven like a writing desk?

ADDI raises her hand.

Ah, yes, you do hear me. Do you speak as well?

ADDI
I don't have my letter.

TEACHER
Which one? A, B, C? D? Q is a nasty one. Never can keep my hands on it. U? Is it U?

ADDI
It *is* me.

RINA
What she means is…we are working on *letter-writing*. Writing letters.

TEACHER
Yes, yes. Writing letters. I know all about them. LMNOP and so forth. That's not all one. It's a bunch. Let's work on writing letters.

RINA
Not *those* kind of letters–

The rumble of a book cart down the hall. The sound of a monstrous insect and impending doom. It is very unpleasant.

TEACHER
Uh oh. Uh oh. Uh oh.
Everyone remain calm.
No one is in trouble. Well, someone is in trouble, but statistically speaking, it's probably not you. Unless it is you. In which case, my most sincere condolences.

Sit. Hands folded. Maybe she won't see us if we are still. Like a dinosaur. I hear some dinosaurs have very bad eyesight.

"Screw your courage to the sticking place," lads and lattices.

It will be bad. Then it will be good. Then it will be not-so-good, then very bad. It will probably be fine in the end.

Unless it's not.

5, 4, 3, 2, –

The teacher points to a door.
The Librarian bursts through like a dragonsnake freight train, trailed by her library aides.

THE LIBRARIAN
Oh why must I descend from where I hide
Amongst the stacks of books I love so well?–

TEACHER (an aside)
LMNOP will have to wait. Not all
one letter. Many letters. All different.

THE LIBRARIAN
Seems someone here has stolen and has lied
Because there is a missing book I smell

This tome contains a danger so severe
And like all books you must treat it with care
For if you open it, you'll d i s a p p e a r
And lose yourself within the pages there

Until I have the book back in my hand
You all may stay all day and watch the clock
The book holds power you don't understand

TEACHER
Pray, what's the name?
LIBRARIAN
It's called *The Jabberwock*.

Lightning strike, thunder or something dramatically similar.
TEACHER
Proceeding as if all is well
Ah, yes, catchy title, that.

(Shuttling the librarian & her entourage out the door as the librarian protests.)

Well, that's all the time we have for creepy librarians at the moment. Must get back to LMNOP. They won't stay in the alphabet all day, after all.

Goodbye, good luck, auf wiedersehen, adieu, may the force be with you.

Closes door behind librarian.

Whew. That was a close one.
Let's not do that again.

Edi raises a hand.

                    EDI
What's *The Jabberwock?*

                　TEACHER
Ah. Yes. Glad you asked. Not really.
A poem. You know them I trust: epic, elegy, couplet. Letters, words, meaning. Rhyme, meter, form. I've got rhythm, I've got music. All of that and tra la la.

                    ADDI
Of course we know poems.

                　TEACHER
But do you. Do you really *know* poems? When did you last meet a poem? What was its name?

RINA
I read that anytime *The Jabberwock* goes missing, strange things happen.

TEACHER
Ah yes. Strange, terrible, bizarre, abnormal, ludicrous, wacky.
Probably has nothing to do with us. Unless it does.

What were we talking about?

ADDI
What kind of strange things happen?

TEACHER
Oh, you know. Folderol and fiddle dee dee. Stuff and nonsense. Things of little consequence. Now—
    Let's have no more talk of poetry,
    Lookingglass books and things,
    "Of shoes, and ships and sealing-wax,
    And whether pigs have wings."

ADDI
What's a Lookingglass book?

TEACHER
Was that your takeaway?

EDI
Yes, what is a looking-glass book?

TEACHER
Who said that?

ADDI
You did.

TEACHER
Well, you can't expect me to think everything I say when I say everything I think.

EDI
But isn't that the same thing?

TEACHER
Yes, of course, a horse is a horse, letters and letters are the same. *That's* what we're talking about.

ADDI
But it's not at all what we're talking about.

TEACHER
Now, who shall begin? (To Rina) You seem to know what you are doing.
Continue doing it.

Rina pops up from her seat.

RINA
How to Write a Letter:

TEACHER
Yes! We are working on letters. ABC. I know them all. All 26, very well in fact. I see them regularly.

RINA
If the Letter is to be in answer to another, begin by getting out that *other* letter and reading it through in order to refresh your memory.

Rina has grown bunny ears.

TEACHER
Very good. Continue! Go on. Etcetera, so on and so forth, ad infinitum.

(To Addi) Hold this, will you?

But whatever you do, *do not open it.*

(Hands Addi The Jabberwock book.)

EDI
Next, address and Stamp the Envelope.

Edi has grown bunny ears.

ADDI
(Examining book) *Wait.*

TEACHER
What! *Before* writing the Letter?

ADDI

(Regarding the book) This is…

EDI

Most certainly. Otherwise, you will go on writing till the last moment, and just in the middle of the last sentence, you will become aware that 'time's up!'

CHARLIE

Time's up!

BEAU

Time's up!

RINA

Time's up.

ADDI

You have the librarian's book!

TEACHER

No I don't.

You have the librarian's book.

ADD STUDENTS

Then comes the hurried wind-up—the wildly-scrawled signature—the hastily-fastened envelope,—

ALL STUDENTS (Cont.)

That way madness lies.

All the students have become bunnies.

ADDI

(To teacher) But I don't want the librarian's book.

TEACHER

(A struggle ensues) You do.

ADDI

I don't.

TEACHER

You do.

ADDI

I don't.

TEACHER

You don't.

ADDI

I do.

TEACHER

You don't.

ADDI

I do.

TEACHER

You don't.

ADDI

I do.

TEACHER

Ah, well, okay then, if you want it, you can have it. But whatever you do, *don't* open it.

ADDI

(*Realizing she's been had*) WAIT.

Bunnies.

TEACHER

Wait. You don't want the book. You want what's *inside* the book. I meant what I said, but I didn't say what I meant.

ADDI

What's inside the book.

Addi sees a bookmark sticking out of the book and slips it out. She opens it.

My – but this is my letter, the assignment – the, the letter I have to write. It's done! It's all written!

The teacher snatches back the letter.

TEACHER

Not a letter, a bookmark.

Bunnies.

ADDI
It's a letter. It's *my* letter.

TEACHER
It is a bookmark when it is marking a book. It is a letter when it is written or read and as it is being *neither* written nor read, it is only a bookmark.

ADDI
But it's all done. Why can't I just – have it?

TEACHER
Oh no no no no no no no. You can't have it. Because you didn't write it yet.
You are still where you began. You haven't gone anywhere. And to get to where you need to be, you need to go where you haven't been.

Bunnies.

ADDI
That doesn't make any sense.

TEACHER
Writing is a journey from point A to point Q.

ADDI
But my letter!

Things are starting to get weird.

ENSEMBLE
Ahhhlice
Ahhhhhhlice
Ahhhhhhliiiice.

The Teacher magically breaks the <u>written</u> letter into five <u>actual</u> letters of the alphabet.

TEACHER

Your *letters*. Because now one letter has become FIVE.

TEACHER (Cont.)	ADDI
A *(Gives it to Rina who runs off as a white rabbit)*	Wait, what are you–-
L *(Gives it to Edi who runs off…)*	Come back here–
I (to Charlie)	Do they –
C (to Beau)	Do they all have bunny ears?
E *(Pinches the E in his/her hand.)*	

ADDI
But those are just letters of the alphabet! They don't mean anything.

TEACHER
Ah, but they mean a great deal.
(A secret) Do you know what writing is?

The Teacher hands her the book. It seems to have gotten a life of its own.

ADDI
The book! It's –it's trying to open! I can't keep it closed!

TEACHER
It's a message in a bottle
That you cast out to sea
To remember who you were
To become who you can be

The Teacher throws the letter E up into the air.

ADDI
WAIT! No!

A million things happen at once:

The book springs open.
Bunnies everywhere.
Alice falls inside.
Letters rain down from the sky.

GO DOWN the RABBIT HOLE

Close your eyes. Allow a deep breath in & a deep breath out. Open. GO. What's on your mind? Words? Pictures? Scribbles? Phrases? Throw it all in the box below.

PART 2: 5 ALICES WEARING THE SAME DRESS

White Rabbit Charlie appears to the side and addresses the audience.

WHITE RABBIT CHARLIE

Put your own name and address, *in full*, at the top of the paper. It is an aggravating thing––I speak from bitter experience––when a friend, staying at some new address, heads his letter "[insert your town]" simply, assuming that you can get the rest of the address from his previous letter, which perhaps you have destroyed.

White Rabbit disappears.

ADDI, **L**OQI, **I**MAGIN, **C**URI, *and* **E**X *tumble from the rabbit hole. This is the first time any of the Alices has seen any of the other Alices. They all mirror each other until they don't.*

ALL

Who are you?

ALL

Who are you?

ALL

I asked you first.

ALL

I'm Alice.

                        ALL

No, I'm Alice.

                        ALL

No, I'm Alice.

                        ADDI

We got a new teacher.

                        LOQI

I was looking for inspiration.

                        IMAGIN

A book sprang open in my hands.

                        CURI

Letters rained from the sky.

                        EX

And I fell inside.

                        ALL

There were a lot of bunnies.
<REACTION>

                        IMAGIN

I'm so glad I'm not the only one who saw them.

They assess each other. Addi does a bold action and tries to throw them, but they all do it simultaneously. She does something else. Again.

ADDI	THE REST
Wah!	Wah!

ADDI	THE REST
Buh duh duh duh duh duh duh duh	Buh duh duh duh duh duh duh duh

ADDI	THE REST
<Roar>	<Roar>

ALL

Okay. ENOUGH!

The Ensemble emerges from the woodwork as it were.

ENSEMBLE

SIIIIIIIIILEEEEEEENCE!

All of the Alices huddle together.

CURI
Whispering

Did you hear that?

EX

That was terrifying.

IMAGIN

What if it's a three-headed monster who eats girls named Alice?

LOQI

That's extremely specific. Yes, it's probably that.

ADDI

Let me at 'em.

ALL but ADDI

WAIT!

CURI

Alice!

ALL but CURI

Yes?

CURI

Might we all agree that we need to be on the same page?

ENSEMBLE

<GROWL>

                    EX

Yes, okay, I will agree to that.

                 IMAGIN

I am ON THE PAGE.

                          LOQI

            That is not unreasonable given the
            circumstances.

                                ADDI

                        Yeah, fine, whatever.

                 ENSEMBLE

<GROWL>

                 IMAGIN

Okay, then. If we are all on the same team, we can't *all* go by "Alice."

                    LOQI

Yes. That is the first rational thing I've heard out of any of our mouths.

                    ADDI

Speak for yourself.

                    LOQI

I do, thank you so much.

EXPAND YOUR VOCABULARY to EXPAND THE WAY YOU THINK!

Match each word with its definition.

1. Adroit
2. Alacritous
3. Amaranthine
4. Lachrymose
5. Loquacious
6. Irascible
7. Idiosyncratic
8. Itinerant
9. Contentious
10. Egregious

a. Peculiar or individual
b. Traveling from place to place
c. Extremely shocking or outrageous
d. Prone to tears
e. Clever or skillful with your body or mind
f. Cheerfully willing
g. Tending to talk a great deal
h. Everlasting, unfading
i. Easily angered
j. Likely to cause an argument

ANSWER KEY:
1–e, 2–f, 3–h, 4–d, 5–g, 6–i, 7–a, 8–b, 9–j, 10–c

PART 3: A MY NAME IS ALICE

White Rabbit Beau appears and addresses the audience.

WHITE RABBIT BEAU

The best subject, to *begin* with, is your friend's last letter. Write with the letter open before you. Answer their questions, and make any remarks their letter suggests. *Then* go on to what you want to say yourself. Your friend is much more likely to enjoy your wit, after their *own* anxiety for information has been satisfied.

White Rabbit disappears.

ENSEMBLE

A!

CURI

"A" what?

ENSEMBLE

A!

IMAGIN

"A" book, "a" chair, "a"–-uh….

ENSEMBLE

A!

EX

What are we supposed to do?

ENSEMBLE

A!

IMAGIN

Is no one going to acknowledge the additional voices in the room?

LOQI

The letter. It's the letter "A."

IMAGIN

Just me then? That tracks.

CURI

What if it's words that begin with "A"?

LOQI

I know lots of words that begin with A.

ADDI

Alive! Ambitious! Ambidextrous! Adaptable! Adroit!

CURI

What does "adroit" mean?

LOQI

Clever or skillful with your body or mind.

ADDI

Ooh, I like that one! That's me! They are all talking about me!

IMAGIN
(Regarding the Ensemble)
I mean, everyone else can see them right?

CURI

What else?

ADDI

Alacritous.

CURI

What does THAT mean?

LOQI

Cheerfully willing.

EX

Not always!

ADDI

Amaranthine!

IMAGIN

Oh, now that's a beautiful word. *Amaranthine*. Say it: *Amaranthine*.

ENSEMBLE
(Sighs)

Amaranthine.

IMAGIN

Whoa.

CURI

What does that mean?

LOQI

Everlasting, unfading. Also: a dark red, purpley color.

IMAGIN

From the mythical amaranth flower which never fades.

IMAGIN & ENSEMBLE

<Sigh.>

ADDI

But most of all <trumpet flare>

ENSEMBLE

ADVENTUROUS!

ADDI

YES! That is absolutely me. I am Adventurous!

ENSEMBLE

L!

ADDI
To Loqi

You seem to know so many words. Why don't you go next?

LOQI

Lovely!

Leery, Lofty, Lonely, Lost.

EX

Those are all sad though.

LOQI
(directed to Ex)

Lachrymose?

EX

I am *not* prone to tears!

ADDI

Okay.

                    EX

You're gonna make me cry!

                    LOQI

Literary?

                    IMAGIN

Very cute.

                    LOQI

Luminescent!

                    CURI

Do you "give off light?"

                    LOQI

Lustrous!

                    ADDI

That means shiny!

                    LOQI

Linguistic!

                    EX

Well, no argument there.

                    LOQI

And *Last* but not *Least*....

ENSEMBLE

Loquacious!

LOQI

That means "tending to talk a great deal."

IMAGIN

We hadn't figured that out yet.

ENSEMBLE

I!

ADDI
(to Imagin)

Your turn!

IMAGIN

Iiiiiiiiiinquisitive.

CURIOUS

What does that mean?

LOQI

Curious!

CURI

That's me that's me that's me!

ADDI

We are on "I" now, not you.

IMAGIN

On me.

ADDI

That's what I said.

LOQI

You said on "I."

ENSEMBLE

S/he means the letter "I"!

EX

OH MY GOSH THE WALLS ARE TALKING!

IMAGIN

Did you *just* notice that!?

EX

I feel so many things. It's a lot to take in.

ADDI

Back to "I" please?

LOQI

I think you mean "you."

ADDI

Not "u."

ENSEMBLE

THE LETTER "I"!

IMAGIN

That's me!

ADDI

Uhhhhhh.

IMAGIN

Intrepid.

CURI

What does *that* mean?

LOQI

Adventurous!

ADDI

Hey! That's me!

ENSEMBLE

It means "adventurous!"

IMAGIN

Irritated! Inventive! Intrigued! Invigorated! Irascible!

LOQI
Easily angered.

IMAGIN
Impulsive.

LOQI
Acts without thinking.

IMAGIN
Idiosyncratic.

LOQI
Peculiar or individual.

IMAGIN

Insightful, impish, incorrigible, itinerant, improvising!

LOQI
Perceptive, mischievous, unruly, traveling from place to place, making it up as you go!

CURI

But what are you really?

IMAGIN

I imagine… I am all of those things.

ENSEMBLE

Imaginative!

IMAGIN

Yes! Imaginative. I am Imaginative!

ENSEMBLE

C!

ADDI
(To Curi)

Your turn.

CURI

What about….what about what about…capable? Courageous? Competent? Clever, compassionate, calm, caring?

And cold?

IMAGIN

Brrrrr.

CURI

Confident? Creative? Colorful?

LOQI

Cranky?

CURI

Curt!

                    IMAGIN

Contradictory!

                     CURI

Contentious!

                     ADDI

Cunning!

                     CURI

Complicated!

                      EX

Clumsy.

                   ENSEMBLE

CURIOUS!

                     CURI

WHAAAAT?

                   ENSEMBLE

CURIOUS!

                     CURI

Am I? I am! I am curious! Am I?

                     ADDI

You are. Trust us.

CURI

I do trust us. Do I?

LOQI

We could be here all day. How many letters are left?

ENSEMBLE

E!

ADDI

(To Ex) That's you.

EX

EEEEEEE!
I FEEL SO MANY THINGS!
Emotional, embarrassed, eager....

CURI

What else?

EX

Euphoric!

ENSEMBLE

Intense happiness or excitement!

EX

Oh, excitement, yes! And and and Egregious?

ENSEMBLE

Extremely shocking or outrageous!

EX

Eh eh eh eh –-Effervescent?

ENSEMBLE

Vivacious or enthusiastic!

EX

Enthusiastic! I'm enthusiastic too! And and and eccentric?

ENSEMBLE

Unconventional and slightly strange!

LOQI

No argument there.

ENSEMBLE

Expressive!

EX

Yes! That's me! I'm Expressive!

ENSEMBLE

A!

      ADDI

Adventurous!

      ENSEMBLE

L!

      LOQI

Loquacious!

      ENSEMBLE

I!

      IMAGIN

Imaginative!

      ENSEMBLE

C!

      CURI

Curious!

      ENSEMBLE

E!

      EX

Expressive!

ENSEMBLE

A-L-I-C-E

A-L-I-C-E

Alice!

Alice!

Alice!

Alice!

FIND INSPIRATION by SHIFTING DIRECTIONS

An acrostic poem repurposes the letters of a word *vertically* to create another poem *horizontally*. Sometimes poets are inspired by a word or line in someone *else's* work to create their own.

For example I could do...

Adventurous　　　　　**A** child who

Loquacious　　　　　**L**oves to

Imaginative　　　　　**I**magine is a

Curious　　　　　**C**loud in the

Expressive　　　　　**E**ye of the storm

Create your own acrostic poems with the the words below!

W　　　　　A
O　　　　　L
N　　　　　I
D　　　　　C
E　　　　　E
R

PART 4: THE HALL OF DOORS

All of the Alices are shaking hands, saying "it's nice to meet you," "a pleasure," "hello," "the pleasure is mine," "nice to meet you," etc.

White Rabbit Rina appears & addresses the audience.

WHITE RABBIT RINA

Please don't fill more than a page and a half with apologies for not having written sooner! No one wants to read that.

White Rabbit Rina disappears.

EX

I'm sorry.

CURI

For what?

EX

I don't know. It's just a general feeling I carry around and feel the need to express from time to time.

IMAGIN

(Posting to Ex) This one's my favorite.

LOQI

We can't have favorites.

CURI

Could we please move on?

                    ADDI
Let's try these doors.

                    LOQI
What doors?

Doors appear.

                    IMAGIN
These doors.

                    CURI
Curiouser and curiouser.

                    ADDI
No time like the present.

                    THE REST
WAIT!

                    ADDI
Oh, come on. How bad can it be?

Addi opens a door and starts through. The other side is a sudden drop through the sky. Sound of whipping wind. She tilts forward and dangles dangerously and the others have to grab onto her to haul her back in. Ad lib., all talk simultaneously to get her back inside.

                    EX
THAT BAD. It can be *that bad.*

LOQI

Perhaps we should discuss before we open any more doors.

IMAGIN

Perhaps we should.

EX

I feel nervous.

ADDI

You are always nervous.

EX

I'm offended!

ADDI

That too.

CURI

What if we wait and discuss? Or – what if we don't?

Curi opens a door. Sudden terrifying ROAR, breath of a giant beast throws her hair back. She closes it.

CURI

What if we don't do that one.

LOQI

PERHAPS, we should discuss.

IMAGIN

Well, I imagine this one can't be that bad.

She approaches the only teeny tiny door.

LOQI

WHY DOES NO ONE LISTEN TO ME?

Imagin opens a teeny tiny itsy bitsy door.

Choirs of angels. Colors. Beauty. Magic.

ALL

Ooooooooh. <Wonder>

ADDI

It looks like–- there's something in there! (Addi spots the "A" from her letter.) We have to go in this one.

EX

We're too big to go in that one.

ADDI

We have to.

OPEN THE PORTAL

PART 5: DRINK ME

WHITE RABBIT EDI appears & addresses the audience.

WHITE RABBIT EDI

Here is a golden Rule to begin with. *Write legibly*. The average temper of the human race would be perceptibly sweetened, if everybody obeyed this Rule! A great deal of the bad writing in the world comes simply from writing *too quickly*. Of course you reply, "I do it to save *time*". A very good object, no doubt: but what right have you to do it at your friend's expense? Isn't *their* time as valuable as yours?

White Rabbit disappears.

Meanwhile, a SMALL VIAL of liquid appears to the Alices with a tag.

The Alices approach the vial and try to read the tag.

CURI

What does it say?

LOQI

It's impossible to read.

VIAL

Drink me.

IMAGIN

Well, good thing it talks then.

                        VIAL

Drink me.

                        ADDI

Did that thing speak? Ask it how we get through that small door!

                        VIAL

Drink me.

                        LOQI

Repetitive if you ask me. You might expand your vocabulary little one. We just did a whole lesson. Weren't you here for the last scene?

                        VIAL

Drink me.

                        CURI

Should we? Should we drink it?

                        LOQI

That's an awful idea.

A moment.

                        ADDI

Let's do it!

ALL

WAIT!

They all freeze.

VIAL

Drink me.

EX

I don't know how I feel about this.

VIAL

Drink me drink me drink me.

LOQI

Let's talk about it, shall we? Hash it out. Weigh our options. We could make a pros and cons list, take a vote.

EX

I feel nervous.

ADDI

What a surprise.

LOQI

See, that's a con. It makes us nervous. I'll write that down. I don't know where. Maybe there's chalk or a white board or something? Does someone have a magic marker or a long ream of paper?

IMAGIN

OH! What if—

ADDI

Here we go.

IMAGIN

What if when we drink it, it makes us turn into wild animals and we have to forage for food and we never turn back into humans until until until a storm comes that sprinkles us with rain from the tears of wildebeests?

LOQI

Well that's oddly specific.

IMAGIN

What if when we drink it, we blow up like balloons and fly away, up up up into the atmosphere until a migrating flock of geese adopts us or or or — what if it's a potion that makes us invisible and for the rest of our lives no matter how much we talk or move or sing or dance no one will ever see us again??

CURI

Where do you come up with these things?

LOQI

I'm sorry. I don't know if those are pros or cons. Does no one have a Ticonderoga or a Precise V5 Pilot Pen? Those are my favorites, you know.

IMAGIN

What if it makes us taste color?

ADDI

LET'S DO IT!

ALL

WAIT.

CURI

Where did it come from?

EX

I feel nervous about it, but I also feel *excited*.

CURI

Did someone put it here?

LOQI

Excited. That's a pro. I think it's one to one at this point. I'd know if I had a Precise V5 Pilot or a dry erase marker or charcoal or something, but here we are.

CURI

Does it say other things?

EX

I want to try it because I don't know what is going to happen, but I also *don't* want to try it because I don't know what's going to happen.

LOQI

"Fear of the unknown." That's a con. That's, well, I think so at least. That's two cons and one pro. Is there a chalkboard? Like an old-fashioned black chalkboard on wheels? Remember clapping erasers? Anyone?

EX

But what's the point of life if we don't try new things?

IMAGIN

What if it makes time speed up or stop completely and we are frozen forever and ever or— or or or— what if it can make us go back in time?

ADDI

Come ON! Let's do it!

LOQI

Dirt? We could write in dirt. If there were a stick. And dirt. Is there a stick?

ADDI

ENOUGH TALKING! I'M DOING IT!

Addi slugs back the vial.

Addi, unsurprisingly, shrinks.

WHOA.

Addi opens the portal and goes through.

FIND FREEDOM
in the FORM

Haiku is a traditional Japanese poetry form with 17 syllables broken up over three lines in 5-7-5. Each syllable is a beat of text. You can count out the rhythm on your fingertips or tap it on a surface.

Write your own!

___ ___ ___ ___ ___

___ ___ ___ ___ ___ ___ ___

___ ___ ___ ___ ___

___ ___ ___ ___ ___

___ ___ ___ ___ ___ ___ ___

___ ___ ___ ___ ___

PART 6: CHESHIRE CAT SMILE

WHITE RABBIT CHARLIE appears and addresses the audience.

WHITE RABBIT CHARLIE

When you have written a letter that you feel may possibly irritate your friend, *put it aside until the next day*. Then read it over again, and imagine it addressed to yourself. This will often lead to you writing it all over again, taking out a lot of the vinegar and pepper, and putting in honey instead, and thus making a *much* more palatable dish!

White rabbit disappears.

Addi stumbles in with the A.

ADDI

It's the letter – the first part of my letter! It's the A.

I got the A!

She looks around, but there is no one.

She tries to call to the other Alices.

I got the A!

The CHESHIRE CAT appears to Addi.

CHESHIRE CAT
The moon is a smile
Or a frown depending on
How you tilt your head

ADDI
Oh, hi, who are you?
CHESHIRE CAT
Why, I am the Cheshire Cat
And who might you be?

ADDI
I'm Alice – or well,–
I was when I got up this
morning, but now I'm –

CHESHIRE CAT
Not sure anymore?
You fell down the rabbit hole.
ADDI
How did you know that?

CHESHIRE CAT
We all fall down the
rabbit hole from time to time.
ADDI
What's a "Cheshire Cat?"

CHESHIRE CAT
Cheshire is a place
Where cream is so delicious
The cats are happy

ADDI
Which way should I go?
CHESHIRE
That depends a great deal on
Where you'd like to *Get*

ADDI
Well, I don't care where!
Loqi rushes through the door, out of breath.
LOQI
I do! I very much care
Where we choose to go.

ADDI
Look at this: the "A!"
LOQI
How ever did you manage
To find it down here?

ADDI
I opened the door
And went through and there it was!
LOQI
Strange, I can't seem to—

CHESHIRE CAT
Speak how you wish to?
That's the magic of haiku
In seventeen beats

ADDI
Haiku? What is s/he—
LOQI
Oh! Of course! 5-7-5
beats of a haiku!

ADDI
That makes seventeen!
LOQI
To the cat
You only speak poetry?
CHESHIRE CAT
It's the only way.

<MEOW>

CHESHIRE CAT (Cont.)

Wonderland is full
Of poets you'll find — isn't
That why you've come here?

ADDI

I opened a book —

LOQI

To find a letter

CHESHIRE CAT

Ah, yes,
Letters — words — meaning

LOQI

Not that kind of let —

CHESHIRE CAT

Words are a window you must
Peer through to find you

The Cheshire Cat disappears.

The "L" falls from the sky.

ADDI

Wha —

LOQI

Look! It's the "L!"

ADDI

Now we have two!

FEEL the RHYTHM

Just like music, language has a rhythm. Iambic pentameter is a form of poetry with 10 syllables per line. The scansion, or the rhythm of a line, is an unstressed syllable followed by a stressed syllable. Looking for the rhythm? Skip around to find it.

For example:

Oh <u>what</u> is <u>this</u> we <u>find</u> here <u>in</u> our <u>midst</u>?

Write your own line. Write a second line and make it rhyme with the first to make a rhyming couplet!

PART 7: ADVICE FROM A CATERPILLAR

White Rabbit Beau appears and addresses the audience.

WHITE RABBIT BEAU

If your friend makes a severe remark, make your reply distinctly *less* severe. If they make a friendly remark, let your reply be distinctly *more* friendly. If, in making up, each friend went *five-eighths* of the way—why, there would be more reconciliations than quarrels!

White Rabbit disappears.

ADDI

Now, what do we do?

LOQI

That was strange. I couldn't talk nearly as much as I wanted to. It was almost as if someone had tied my tongue up. Oh, look, no more constraints on language. What a relief.

ADDI

For who exactly?
Imagin runs on.

IMAGIN

Thank goodness I've found you!

ADDI

How did you get here?

IMAGIN

I drank the potion and shrunk, same as you.

LOQI

Wonderful.

ADDI

Where's the fire?

IMAGIN

Well, I was wondering...is this real?

The caterpillar assembles from many parts and threads its way around the Alices.

LOQI

Are you referring to the enormous predatory insect that's threading its way around us threateningly at this very moment?

IMAGIN

That would be exactly what I'm referring to.

ADDI

I guess this is what we're doing next.

IMAGIN

I was hoping it was just my imagination.

The caterpillar encircles the Alices.

THE CATERPILLAR
Menacing

To pass the time in search of sustenance
Is such a weary way to fill one's days
When every teeny speech and utterance
Brings me to tears a million different ways

IMAGIN	ADDI	LOQI
Oh dear oh dear oh dear.	I thought caterpillars were friendly?	Well, this is just wonderful. I told you we shouldn't have taken that potion.

THE CATERPILLAR

                Oh what is this we find here in our midst?
                A child, or not a child and child again
(to Addi)   Adventure-seeking is the throne she sits
(to Loqi)   Where this one wields her mouth in lieu of
                      pen

LOQI

Well I—

THE CATERPILLAR
To Imagin
But this one is by far the most advanced

LOQI

<Scoff>

THE CATERPILLAR

Her mind will never break before it bends
So tell me dear, who are you by expanse
Before our time is up and night descends

IMAGIN

We thank you very kindly for your time

ADDI
Whispered to Loqi

What is she doing?

IMAGIN

And hope we have not stumbled in your lair

LOQI
Whispered back to Addi

She's speaking like it. How is she speaking like it?

IMAGIN

You clearly trade so eloquent with rhyme
We'll quickly leave and get out of your hair

They try to leave.

The caterpillar does not let them go.

THE CATERPILLAR

Not so fast my scrumptious little friends
I'll let you leave in time if I decide
But first before you meet your bitter end
You must prevail me who, how, where, what, why

IMAGIN

Well —

THE CATERPILLAR

And not just you, you know the rhythm dear
But also, lo, your friends must speak their piece
And I will wait and listen to your queer
And querulous debate before I eat

The Alices urgently huddle.

ADDI

What the heck is going on?

LOQI

Oh no.

ADDI

What?

LOQI

We speak how that thing speaks and we get to go.

ADDI

How?

IMAGIN

It's iambic pentameter, don't you hear?

(Counting the rhythm on her fingers) daDUM daDUM daDUM daDUM daDUM

ADDI

What is iambic pentameter?

IMAGIN

It's a form of poetry. It has to do with a certain amount of syllables.

LOQI

Like that cat.

ADDI

It's like math and literature had a baby. Uuuhhhhh, my brain.

IMAGIN

It is. It is! Okay. Ten syllables create a line. Each line is an unstressed syllable followed by a stressed syllable and so on. daDUM. That is one meter. One meter is two syllables. And 2 x 5 = 10. Each line is 10 syllables.

ADDI

Could you– could you go over that one more time?

Rewind.

IMAGIN
Repeating just like before

Ten syllables create a line. Each line is an unstressed syllable followed by a stressed syllable and so on. daDUM. That is one meter. One meter is two syllables. And 2 x 5 = 10. Each line is 10 syllables.

LOQI
In reference to the rewind

Well that was unexpected.

ADDI

Whoa.

LOQI

Perhaps we could rewind further to the time before we fell down this dank rabbit hole and drank a questionable substance that has clearly set us on a path to certain and inevitable destruction?

A moment.

No? Worth a shot.

The Caterpillar growls.

ADDI
regrouping

But what was it saying?

IMAGIN

We have to answer her questions: who, how, where, what, why or, uh – she will eat us.

LOQI

Well that is just great. Well done, us.

Another growl from The Caterpillar.

ADDI

<Whelp>

LOQI

Okay, okay, 10 syllables. Unstressed followed by stressed. I suddenly feel very motivated.

ADDI

I have no idea what I'm doing.

IMAGIN

It's the rhythm of the human heart. daDUM daDUM daDUM daDUM daDUM.

ADDI

If the endings also rhymed?

IMAGIN

Yes.

LOQI

What's next, Villanelle? Ekphrastic? Why don't we all construct some pithy Limericks while we are at it?

IMAGIN
To Loqi, shoving her forward

Why don't you start? You love talking so much.

LOQI

    Your Caterpillar-ness, you've asked us all
    The Who, we are but Alice thrice appeared
    The How, we drank and went from big to small
    The Where, why, where is easy: we are here

IMAGIN

    The What, we chased a rabbit down a hole
    While in a classroom well before we shrank
    Some letters, we were writing, but he stole
    And came upon a cat, who we must thank

It is Addi's turn. Addi is lost.

> IMAGIN (cont)
> *Prompting Addi*

And Why...

> ADDI

> oh why, oh why oh why oh why
> That is a question curiously posed
> (I feel my palms are wet; my mouth is dry
> The room, it spins beneath my whirling nose)

> THE CATERPILLAR
> *Menacing*

> You answer Who and Where and What and How
> But still you have to answer one time more
> Or I will feast upon *three* Alice now
> So tell me quick and I'll show you the door

Uh oh. Addi is sunk.

Curi appears to save the day. Dah duh dah dah!

> CURI

> The Why – why that's MY question, glad you asked
> Where once were three, are now before you four
> We'll answer all the queries you have tasked
> And leave you with a dozen queries more

> For I am much more curious by far
> Than all your questions multiplied by ten
> So who are you, I wonder, when and how,
> You plan to make your curious descent

                    CURI (cont.)
>   *Why* is the biggest question that there is
>   Why are we here? Why do we live – and how
>   Do you suppose we answer you with this:
>   Why don't you metamorph yourself right now?

The caterpillar combusts into a million butterflies.
An "I" falls from the sky.
All are stunned.

                    IMAGIN

How did you do that?

                    ADDI

That was awesome.

                    CURI

What's this?

                    ADDI

It's another letter!

                    IMAGIN

It's an "I! I got the "I"!

                    ADDI
                    (To Curi)

Look, we've got three! That's good right? That must be good.

LOQI

How did you get here— and just in time too?

CURI

I drank the potion and shrunk

CURI, IMAGIN, ADDI

— same as you.

ADDI

Three down; two to go!

LOQI

Great. Just great. A Painfully Perplexing Potion, A Philosophical Floating Feline, and a Condescending Carnivorous Caterpillar. What's next, some Sagacious Sorcerer set to Sting us with a Sonnet?

IMAGIN

Very nice use of alliteration.

LOQI

I wasn't even trying.

ADDI

I'm not sure if that's a good thing.

CURI

Wanna see something strange?

IMAGIN

Stranger than that?

ADDI

Totally.

FIND MEANING in REPETITION
FIND MEANING in REPETITION
FIND MEANING in REPETITION

What's your favorite line in the play? Write it 3 times.

Do you notice something over and over in your life? An animal? A person? A place?

Does a phrase come up again and again in your day? An image?

PART 8: WE'RE ALL MAD HERE

The Mad Hatter & Ensemble host a never-ending tea party. It is chaos.
Addi, Loqi, Imagin and Curi take in the craziness.

White Rabbit Rina addresses the audience.

WHITE RABBIT RINA

Don't repeat yourself. When once you have said your say, fully and clearly, on a certain point, and have failed to convince your friend, *drop that subject*: to repeat your arguments, over and over again, you will become a Circulating Decimal.

Did you ever know a Circulating Decimal come to an end?

White Rabbit Rina disappears.

IMAGIN

What are we looking at?

ADDI

Who cares? What do you think we have to do to get the next letter?

CURI

Can I introduce you to…the Mad Hatter?

LOQI

Who? Who is the Mad Hatter?

THE MAD HATTER

I am the Mad Hatter!

ENSEMBLE 2

I am the Mad Hatter.

ENSEMBLE 3

I am the Mad Hatter.

ENSEMBLE 4 & 5

I am the Mad Hatter.

ENSEMBLE 6, 7 & 8

I am the Mad Hatter.

ADDI

I AM THE MAD HATTER.

LOQI

Not you. You're not—
Come on! This is insanity.

CURI

You know what they say about insanity?

ENSEMBLE

It's doing the same thing over and over and expecting a different result!

ENSEMBLE

I am the Mad Hatter!
I am the Mad Hatter!
I am the Mad Hatter!

LOQI

Stop it, all of you. All of you can't be the Mad Hatter.

ENSEMBLE & the ALICES

I am the Mad Hatter!

ADDI

Oh no.

CURI

Oops.

IMAGIN

It is kind of contagious.

LOQI

We are going to pretend this never happened. We will never speak of it again.

ADDI

That's going to be hard for you.

IMAGIN

Maybe we should go. It feels like this whole place is just trying to consume us in some way or other.

ADDI

But we have to do this. I just know it. We have to get the next letter here.

LOQI

Don't you see? That's how they get you. First it's all simple haiku with a Harmless House cat and before you know it, it's like Spartacus threw the worst tea party ever.

Tapping of glasses.

THE MAD HATTER

Speech!

ENSEMBLE 2

Speech speech!

ENSEMBLE

Speech speech! Speech speech!

LOQI

Let's go. No one makes good speeches. They go on and on, circumnavigating the point until everyone stops listening, praying for it to end. Or death. Whichever comes first.

ADDI

I kind of have to agree. Let's go.

Rewind.
They repeat exactly as before.

THE MAD HATTER

I am the Mad Hatter.

ENSEMBLE 2, 3, 4

I am the Mad Hatter.

ENSEMBLE & the ALICES *(they can't help themselves)*

I am the Mad Hatter.

ADDI

Oh no.

CURI

Oops.

IMAGIN

It is kind of contagious.

LOQI

We are going to pretend this never happened. We will never speak of it again.

ADDI

That's going to be hard for you.

####### IMAGIN

Maybe we should go. It feels like this whole place is just trying to consume us in some way or other.

####### ADDI

But we have to do this. I just know it. We have to get the next letter here.

####### LOQI

Don't you see? That's how they get you. First it's all simple haiku with a Harmless House cat and before you know it, it's like Spartacus threw the worst tea party ever —

Record skip.

####### CURI

Wait. Haven't we done this before?

####### ENSEMBLE

Speech speech! Speech speech!

####### IMAGIN

We've definitely done this before.

####### ENSEMBLE

Speech speech! Speech speech!

LOQI

Anyone want to go back to the Impossibly Ill-tempered Insect?

ADDI

I think... I think we have to make a speech.

IMAGIN

So make a speech.

LOQI

No one makes good speeches. They go on and on, circumnavigating the point until –wait. Did I already say that?

IMAGIN

Oh my gosh, this is like staring at the ceiling at 3AM rehashing the poor choices of your day over and over and –-

LOQI

I'm going back to the bug.

ALICES

WAIT!

ENSEMBLE

Speech speech! Speech speech!

ADDI

Look, we just have to make a speech. *(To Curi)* Why don't you do it? You brought us here.

CURI

What am I supposed to say?

The Jabberwock book appears.

IMAGIN

Look! A magical book!

LOQI

That's not suspicious at all.

ADDI

(recognizing the book) It's *The Jabberwock!*

ENSEMBLE

The Jabberwock! The Jabberwock!

IMAGIN

This! This is your speech! *(Referencing the book.)*

CURI

Kind of like a flask of unidentifiable liquid presenting itself and saying "drink me?"

LOQI

That worked out so well for us.

ADDI

Don't you see? It's the Lookinglass book.

CURI

What's that?

LOQI

Stuff and nonsense. It's illegible. This whole place is upside-down.

IMAGIN

Not upside-down. Look! Backwards. It's backwards! Is there…is there a mirror?

ENSEMBLE

A mirror! A mirror! My kingdom for a mirror!

The stage divides as if split by a mirror with Curi, Addi and 1/2 the ensemble on one side; Imagin, Loqi and the other 1/2 of the ensemble on the other side. Throughout the following, they mirror each other.

CURI & IMAGIN
Reading

'Twas brillig, and the slithy toves
    Did gyre and gimble in the wabe:

LOQI & ADDI

All mimsy were the borogoves,
    And the mome raths outgrabe.

ALL

"Beware the Jabberwock, my son!
   The jaws that bite, the claws that catch!
Beware the Jubjub bird, and shun
   The frumious Bandersnatch!"

CURI & IMAGIN

He took his vorpal sword in hand;
   Long time the manxome foe he sought—

ALICES

So rested he by the Tumtum tree
   And stood awhile in thought.

1/3 ENSEMBLE

And, as in uffish thought he stood,
   The Jabberwock, with eyes of flame,

2/3 ENSEMBLE

Came whiffling through the tulgey wood,
   And burbled as it came!

ALL

One, two! One, two! And through and through
   The vorpal blade went snicker-snack!
He left it dead, and with its head
   He went galumphing back.

CURI & IMAGIN

"And hast thou slain the Jabberwock?
   Come to my arms, my beamish boy!

ENSEMBLE

O frabjous day! Callooh! Callay!"

ALICES

He chortled in his joy.

ENSEMBLE

'Twas brillig, and the slithy toves
    Did gyre and gimble in the wabe:
All mimsy were the borogoves,
    And the mome raths outgrabe.

Sound of clock alarms, chimes.

ENSEMBLE

Tea time tea time tea time tea time!
Tea time tea time tea time tea time!

The "C" appears. Maybe it falls from the sky. Maybe it is poured from a teapot into a cup. Maybe it's in the book. Be creative with how the letters appear.

ADDI

Look Look Look!

IMAGIN

What is it?

CURI

It's the "C"!

ADDI

We only need one more!

BE CURIOUS

What are you curious about? Circle all the things you are curious about below.

NATURE	BOOKS	ART
LANGUAGE	SCIENCE	GEMSTONES
HISTORY	POETRY	ANIMALS
DANCE	MUSIC	INSTRUMENTS
ATHLETICS	WRITING	TRAVEL
FOOD	OUTER SPACE	DESIGN
PAINTING	SCULPTING	PHOTOGRAPHY
SINGING	SWIMMING	YOGA
MEDITATION	WELLNESS	MAGIC

What *else* are you curious about?

_____   _____

_____   _____

_____   _____

_____   _____

_____   _____

PART 9: GO ASK ALICE

Chaos and celebration continue from the previous scene. *If you want an opportunity to sell concessions, here is your chance. Have bunnies take to the aisles calling "Get your popcorn, get your peanuts! Fresh water!" "Welcome to the Queen's Court!" "Let the games begin!" Etc.

The Queen appears with the four White Rabbits.
EX is the Queen.
Surprise.

EX as QUEEN

SILENCE!!!!
All fall to the ground, silent.

THE WHITE RABBITS

If doubtful whether to end with "yours faithfully," or "yours truly," or "yours most faithfully, truly, madly, deeply," refer to your correspondent's last letter, and make your winding-up *at least as friendly as theirs*; in fact, even a shade *more* friendly, it will do no harm!

ENSEMBLE

The queen does not like to be kept waiting.

ADDI
(To the rabbits)

There you are! You're all the reason we're in this mess, you little–

She goes after the rabbits.

      CURI

Wait, you're the queen?

     EX as QUEEN

Whooo is asking?

      IMAGIN

This is weird. Does anyone else think this is weird?

      CURI

Aren't you one of us?

      ADDI

This is weird. *(To rabbits)* Get back here! I want my—

      LOQI

How did you get here?

      ADDI

How do you think? She drank the potion and shrunk

      ALICES

Same as—

   EX as QUEEN & ENSEMBLE

SILEEEEENCE!

THE WHITE RABBITS

The queen would play a game!

ENSEMBLE

A game a game the queen would play a game!

ADDI
(after the rabbits again)

Have you heard of the hungry caterpillar?

EX as QUEEN & ENSEMBLE

SILEEEEEEENCE!

The following White Rabbit language can be choral or divided amongst the rabbits.

THE WHITE RABBITS

In this corner, Her Majesty, the Expressive, Emotional, Effervescent and Effulgent–

LOQI
In confidence to other Alices
That means radiant.

ADDI
Thank you. Thank you so much.

THE WHITE RABBITS

–the Enthusiastic, Electric, Emboldened, Engaging

CURI
What is going on?

IMAGIN

I think we are going to play a game or fight to the death. Outlook unclear.

THE WHITE RABBITS

—the Empowered, Energetic, Ecstatic and Enraged, The Queen of Wonderland.

ENSEMBLE

<Cheer>

ADDI

I do not like our odds.

THE WHITE RABBITS

And in this corner:

Alice.

LOQI

Well, that was a rousing endorsement.

ADDI

(To other Alices) But isn't she one of us?

IMAGIN

Apparently not anymore.

CURI

(To Loqi) Didn't you say this place has been trying to consume us this whole time?

THE WHITE RABBITS

Let the game begin!

IMAGIN

(To the Alices) What if it's...succeeding?

ENSEMBLE

<Cheer>

CURI

(To the Queen) What kind of game are we to play?

QUEEN

Do you know the game of questions?

ADDI

Yeah, we know questions.

ENSEMBLE

<EEEEH= buzzer sound>

ADDI

What was that?

THE WHITE RABBITS

Statement. One for the Queen.

ADDI

Were we already playing?

QUEEN

Did you hear that sound of you losing *question mark?*

ADDI

I didn't know we were playing!

ENSEMBLE

<EEEEH>

THE WHITE RABBITS

Whiny retort. Two for the queen; zero for Alice.

ADDI

Who are you calling "whiny," you little—-?

QUEEN

Do you know what happens at three?

Addi goes to speak, but Curi silences Addi.

Ding ding ding!

WHITE RABBITS

Opponents to your corners.

The Alices huddle.

CURI
Don't you get it? It's a game of questions.

ADDI
What's that?

IMAGIN
Everything we say has to be in the form of a question. If we make a statement, we lose.

ADDI
What happens if we lose?

CURI
Do you really want to find out?

IMAGIN
(To Addi)
You shouldn't talk and (to Loqi) you *definitely* shouldn't talk.

LOQI
Me? What did I do? See? Those were questions. I can do questions.

IMAGIN
Oh please, you wax on and on

about your opinions. No one can get a word in edgewise.

            LOQI
I don't think that that's necessarily—-

            IMAGIN
            (to Addi)
And you—

                    ADDI
What did *I* do?

            IMAGIN

You are the queen of one-liners. No. Neither of you can talk.

Ding ding ding!

Round 2.

(To Curi) You handle this.

            LOQI
Fine.

                    ADDI
                    Whatever.

They unhuddle.

QUEEN

(To rabbit) My dear rabbits, could you refresh our memories since our guests took an eon to confer with each other?

THE WHITE RABBITS

Yes, your majesty.

"How to Write a Letter:
If the Letter is to be in answer to another,–

QUEEN

Could you, perhaps, skip to the relevant part, please?

THE WHITE RABBITS

Certainly, your Majesty.

<Eh hem>

The rabbits play-act all of the other characters.

R: (As Queen) Do you know the game of questions?

E: (As Addi) Yeah, we know questions.

CB: (As Ensemble) <EEEEH>

E: (As Addi) What was that?

B (As him/herself) Statement. One for the Queen.

E: (As Addi) Were we already playing?

R:(As Queen) Did you hear that sound of you losing *question mark?*

E: (As Addi) I didn't know we were playing!

CB: (As Ensemble) <EEEEH>

B (As him/herself) Whiny retort. Two for the queen; zero for Alice.

E: (As Addi) Who are you calling "whiny," you little—-?

R:(As Queen) Do you know what happens at three?

QUEEN
Resuming game

(To rabbit) Well, aren't you useful?

Ding ding ding. Round 2.

QUEEN (cont.)

(To the Alices) So, are we all up to speed?

CURI

(To Queen) What happens at three

—-your Majesty?

QUEEN

Why do you ask?

CURI

Don't you know?

QUEEN

What did you say?

CURI

Are you having trouble hearing?

QUEEN

Could you speak up?

CURI

IS THIS A GOOD VOLUME?

QUEEN

WHY ARE YOU SCREAMING AT ME?

CURI
whispering

Would you prefer I whisper?

QUEEN

Yes, that's much —

ENSEMBLE

<EEEEH>

THE WHITE RABBITS

Statement sentence construct. One for Alice. The Queen is still in the lead.

QUEEN
angry

Why did you do that?!

CURI

What?

QUEEN

Why did you make me lose?

CURI

Do you want to win?

QUEEN

Don't we all?

CURI

Isn't the saying, "It's not whether you win or lose, but how you play the game?"

QUEEN

Why did you say that?

CURI

Does that bother you?

QUEEN

Why do you care?

                              CURI

Does it matter?

                             QUEEN

What if it does?

                              CURI

To who?

                             QUEEN
                           Losing it

TO WHOM!

                           ENSEMBLE

<EEEH>

Ding ding ding!

                       THE WHITE RABBITS

Syntactical correction *exclamation point*. Alice two; Queen two.
End of round 2!

The Queen roars.

Ding ding ding. Round 3.

                             QUEEN

Why are you making me SO ANGRY?

CURI

Am I?

QUEEN

Who do you think you are?

ALL the ALICES

Who do you think *you* are?

ENSEMBLE

<Doo doo doo doo = warning sound>

THE WHITE RABBITS

Warning. Repetition. Two warnings is one strike. Three strikes loses the game. The Queen is ahead by a hair.

>ADDI *to others*
>We need one more letter.
>We just have to say!

>CURI
>But if you're playing yourself

>IMAGIN
>Don't you lose either way?

THE WHITE RABBITS

Your Majesty?

      ADDI
      Addi has an idea.

Or what if…?

      QUEEN

Why don't you begin, *Alice*?

Addi steps forward, holds up her letter. Loqi does the same, followed by Imagin & Curi.

They form the text: A-L-I-C-

    ADDI, LOQI, IMAGIN, CURI

Who are you?

      QUEEN
    The queen is thrown

Who – am I?

Ding ding ding.

She discovers an E somewhere – perhaps embedded on her hand or plucked midair.

I'm – I'm– why, I'm–

THE QUEEN adds the E to make A-L-I-C-E.

Suddenly, everything changes.

ENSEMBLE:

Ahhhhlice.

Ahhhhhhlice.

Ahhhhhhhlice.

CREATE your own
MESSAGE IN A BOTTLE

What advice would you give your older or younger self?

Dear_____,

Yours most Faithfully,
Truly, Madly, Deeply,

_____

PART 10: ALICE ALL ALONG
Magically back to the classroom, the first moment of the show, but the Mad Hatter is present as The Teacher.

ALL

ALICE!

Addi is on top of the desk, reaching up, as if she just caught her letter falling.

ADDI

Yes? What? Yes?

The classroom scene freezes.

Over the following section, Loqi, Imagin, Curi and Ex all recede, like the tide.

LOQI

When you take your letters to the Post Office, *carry them in your hand.*

IMAGIN

If you put them in your pocket you will take a long walk, passing the Post-Office *twice,*

CURI

going and returning, going and returning, and when you get home,

                              EX
they will still be in your pocket.

Loqi, Imagin, Curi and Ex pull audience members' letters from their pockets.

The classroom unfreezes.

                    ADDI
Did someone say something?

          RINA
You're next, Alice.
                    EDI
          Your letter, remember?
                              CHARLIE
                    Go, get 'em tiger.
                              BEAU
                    It'll be great. Or not.
                    Either way, it'll be okay.

                    TEACHER
Alice! Did you find it?

The <audience text> below is the "Advice to a Young Caterpillar" text the audience submits at top of show.

          LOQI
<audience text>
                    ADDI
Did I–?

The Janitor (Cheshire Cat) materializes.

                THE JANITOR
       Sometimes you must be
       Lost in order to be found
       Have you been searching?

    IMAGIN
\<audience text\>

                ADDI
Have I–?

The Librarian materializes.

                THE LIBRARIAN
Perhaps you've lost yourself, perhaps you've found
The message in a bottle that you send
Now if you've charted When, Why, Where and How
I wonder this: Who are you at the end?

    CURI
\<audience text\>

                ADDI
I think. I think… it found me.
Addi is holding the book with the letter tucked inside.

    EX
\<audience text\>

Addi opens the book and retrieves the letter. She hands the book to the Teacher who hands it to the Librarian. She opens the letter and reads.

ADDI

Oh, to be the person you've discovered
By journeying the shores inside your soul
Writing, the reward you have uncovered
A message in a bottle that you hold

The ink is but the shadow that you leave
A mark to show the person you've become
By wrestling your demons as you cleave
The parts of who you were the winning sum

It's who you are, a gift upon the page,
The *journey* is the point of all the stress
To grapple with the questions of an age
to make some sense of all of the duress

Reveal yourself: the gorgeous and grotesque—
It's why a raven's like a writing desk.

She looks to the Mad Hatter/Teacher.
The Mad Hatter nods.

She throws the letter up in the air.
It turns into a raven.
Sound of a raven caw.

All — sharp INHALE of inspiration.

Lights.

END OF PLAY

DRAW your own
CONCLUSION

A sonnet is a poem consisting of 14 lines written in iambic pentameter. The one on the last page is called a Shakespearean Sonnet. A Shakespearean Sonnet is arranged in three quatrains (four-line stanzas) and ends with a couplet (two-line stanza).
The rhyme scheme is ABAB CDCD EFEF GG.

Kate Brennan (playwright) is an artist, educator & creator. She has written a dozen plays and musicals and has taught across the country. She has been named a three-time O'Neill Semifinalist, a Princess Grace Finalist, a Judith Royer Finalist, a Jane Chambers Finalist, and a Cultural Alliance Artist Innovator Award Finalist. Kate is a Designated Linklater Teacher and holds an MFA from UVA. Publications include: *The Ocean of Emotion, Check-In: A Little Book to Practice Presence, A is for Anxiety: A Primer for Parenting through the Apocalypse, How to Dramadoodle* and *ALiEN8*. She is part of the Jonathan Larson Grant Finalist musical-writing team Brennan & White. Substack: *More Humor More Humanity.* www.katebrennan.org

Gregory DeCandia (director) is a community dramaturg. He investigates story, excavate truths and forges community through art. He has worked in many facets of the arts —as an Equity actor, teaching artist, artistic director, designer, playwright, deviser, high school teacher, college professor, podcast-creator & more. www.gregorydecandia.com

Wrenee Murphy (cover art) is a mixed media & collage artist whose work invites viewers into a world of hidden meanings, layered textures, and emotional resonance—where wonder, resilience, and imagination collide. Drawing on lived experience and subconscious excavation, she weaves together symbols, textures, and found imagery into richly expressive compositions. Her dreamlike and surreal art explores memory, transformation, and self-reclamation. For "The Wonder In Alice" project, Wrenee reimagines Wonderland as a journey inward, offering an invitation to make meaning from mystery and reclaim one's sense of wonder. wreneemurphyart.com

www.ingramcontent.com/pod-product-compliance
Lightning Source LLC
LaVergne TN
LVHW011209080426
835508LV00007B/685